ANTLER BASKETS

... Weaving Rocky Mountain Memories

text and illustrations
by
Bobi Marshall Harris

Photography
by
Michael C. Stewart

■ ACKNOWLEDGMENTS

Many special people contributed to this project in so many ways. So thank you to the students and friends who offered so much encouragement and advice. Thank you to Lori M. Newman, who helped me with the editing. Thank you to my family who mowed around the honeysuckle and rescued antlers from the dog. And thank you to the photographer, Mike Stewart, whose pictures really are worth a thousand words.

But most of all, I thank the Grand Creator who fills the earth with treasures and gives us the life to enjoy them.

I enjoy baskets immensely.

Baskets are woven from nature in beautiful shapes and can serve us well. People who merely decorate with a handcrafted basket never truly understand its worth. A special relationship develops when a basket is assigned a function. I know of such a basket. It was used and passed down for generations, and is still in use today.

"It was my Mama's mending basket," the old woman told me as a faraway smile lit up her ancient face. "Many's the night she sat up with this tired ol' thing, patchin' my dresses by the light from our oil lamp. She told me it was her mama's before that."

The old woman held the precious bit of family history proudly on her lap: a small unpretentious thing, with years accumulated between the rows, and the rim dissolving. The basketmaker is long gone, but her creation has remained and may serve many more generations.

The role of baskets in this country has changed since the creation of that little mending basket. With the increased manufacture of paper, plastic and cardboard containers, the demand for the sturdy gathering and storage baskets has diminished.

In recent years, the purpose of baskets has evolved from functional to aesthetic. The primary consideration of most modern basket purchasers is whether or not a basket will complement their decor. This is quite a change from the days—not so long ago—when a basket was woven or bought with strength and function in mind.

This shift in basketry requirements has freed contemporary basketmakers to express their artistic individualities with a wider range of shapes, colors, and designs. It also allows for innovative combinations of weaving materials that may not have been used when strength and durability were prime considerations. Although created largely to be pleasing to the eye, a modern basket is still capable of providing a service to its owner, albeit a less strenuous one than that of the old rural field baskets of our forefathers.

I enjoy weaving those traditional, more serviceable baskets. When a grocery bag rips open, spilling its contents on the ground, I find myself with a strong urge to weave an English willow market basket. But when I am enjoying the scenic beauty of Montana's Rocky Mountains, I want to capture the great outdoors in my baskets. So I gather up pieces of the actual scenery to use as my palette in "painting" the white blankets of snow, the deep green forests, and the reds and oranges of bare branches. I strive to hold the essence of the mountains in my basket.

The antler baskets in this book are the result of my sojourns to the Rockies. They are just a few of the antler baskets I've created and an even smaller portion of the total number of baskets of all types that I've woven over the years.

A weaver with only limited experience in rib-type baskets can weave a simple tube basket (Chap. 5). An advanced basketmaker can perhaps use my examples as a springboard to develop his or her own designs. If you don't have access to antlers, see Chapter 3—or you may substitute sturdy tree limbs or driftwood.

When you weave with natural materials and you love handmade objects, you can hardly be disappointed in your finished basket. After all, even the crudest creation still has plenty of country charm!

--B.M.H.

Missoula, Montana

April 1989

CONTENTS

1 ■ THE BEGINNING

Every spring thousands of deer, elk and moose naturally shed their antlers. And every spring, as a basketmaker in northwestern Montana, I search for these discarded treasures. I gather wild willow and red osier dogwood from along icy streams. I also harvest honeysuckle vines, supple chokecherry, alder, or mountain maple limbs, and deer moss from the branches of tall pine trees.

My excursions into the woods to forage for antlers and other weaving materials are reprieves from the frantic pace of modern living. When I reluctantly turn toward home, I know I am not leaving the mountains entirely. The natural fragrance and serenity of the woods accompany me in the bits and pieces of the forest I carry home. A basket woven with this rustic assortment will hold peaceful memories in every fiber.

At home by the welcoming fire, I begin my special project. First, I select an antler and admire its smooth, strong limbs curving gracefully to tapered ends. Antlers grow in just over four months and serve their bearers well until a new pair forces the old antlers to fall onto the forest floor. Some antlers lay there undisturbed for years while others are nibbled on by forest creatures who find them a tasty source of protein. Occasionally, even a deer will gnaw on a shed horn. The antler I hold in my hands will become the focal point in a basket full of Rocky Mountain memories.

I turn the antler this way and that until I can envision willow ribs circling around and through the perfect handle. When I do, I must interrupt the mountain serenity with a noisy tool: my power drill. Holes must be drilled through the hard bone for the ribs to pass through. While others in the house may find the whine of such a modern implement annoying, I am oblivious to the disturbance. My mind is far away, beginning the journey which will take the special basket in my imagination from concept to reality.

2 ■ WHERE TO FIND ANTLERS

Antlers are shed yearly in a natural process. Deer, elk, and moose do not have to die to provide us with their "horns", so I hope you won't feel bad about using them in a basket. Here are some suggestions to find antlers:

- Advertise in your local paper that you buy shed antlers.

- When displaying at an art or craft show, you might display a sign: "I Buy Antlers".

- If game winter on a farmer's land, he may be glad to have someone else pick up shed horns before they puncture tractor tires. Obtain permission first.

- Check with the Fish and Game Department in your area. They may be able to suggest the best places to go horn hunting in the spring. Be sure the area is open to the general public.

- Taxidermy shops—mismatched or "plain" antlers aren't usually suited for a trophy. They may have some to sell.

- Wild Game Processors—they won't be naturally shed and may need a cleanup.

SUPPLIERS:

Red Barn Baskets
4741 White Street
Missoula, MT 59802
(406) 728-2878

Antlers, native basket
materials. Please send SASE.

Royalwood Ltd.
517 Woodville Road
Mansfield, Ohio 44907
(419) 526-1630

Send $1.00 refundable
for catalog.

Photo courtesy of The Missoulian

3 ■ GATHERING YOUR OWN MATERIALS

Gathering my own basketry materials is the result of my love for the woods and my passion for the past. I began life in New Jersey and was enchanted by the colonial influences that surrounded me there. The restored historical village of Williamsburg was where I first fell in love with another century's lifestyle.

My grandparents' 200-year-old farm also held a great fascination for me. It was there that I led my sisters and brother on explorations of the old smokehouse, the barns, and the carriage house. We climbed over crumbling stone walls and pumped water from the ancient old well. But best of all, my grandmother showed me that the woods were full of treasures.

On our woodland excursions, my grandmother and I searched first for a good, stout walking stick. Somehow, having the "perfect" stick always made the journey more fun. The next discoveries would be wild berries, nuts, and May apples. Then we found fragrant wild flowers that we gathered by the armful. The flowers helped preserve that memorable adventure by adorning the dinner table. A few special blossoms were saved forever, pressed between the leaves of a thick book.

Years later, in the suburbs of the Midwest, I continued my quest for woodland treasures. Thus it took me a long time to walk home from school because I was forever taking detours. I crawled through culverts to follow the creek as it passed under the road home. I meandered through apple orchards. I filled my pockets and lunch box with interesting seeds, sticks and stones. Assigning a great value to my collection, I hid my loot in dresser drawers. My Mom, being a good mother, didn't like all that "dirty stuff" hanging around my clean clothes. But she understood my fascination with—and affection for—nature and never threw my treasures away. Instead, she taught me how to turn my findings into something useful.

Now that I have a home of my own, I am no longer limited to storing my rustic collection in one small dresser drawer. Willow and cattail soak in the bathtubs. Grapevine waits in the freezer. Honeysuckle simmers on the stove. Bundles of wheat and garlic hang on the wall. And you should see the floor—that's what my family would like to do!

But one thing hasn't changed. I still have to turn my treasures into useful items in order to keep the woods indoors. As a result, there are currently 78 baskets in my living room, 102 more on the porch, and over 5,000 in various homes all over this country!

THINGS IN NATURE YOU CAN USE

Collecting your own weaving fibers should not be regarded as work. For me, it's an essential part of being a basket maker. The forests, meadows, and mountains are refreshing and inspire creativity. The search is exciting. You'll never go home empty handed if you keep your eyes open and use your imagination. Don't worry about "rules", try anything once. If it bends a little, it can be ribs. If it bends a lot, use it for weavers. If it doesn't bend at all, try soaking or boiling. If it's just a little doo-dad, tie it on, weave it in, or if you must, glue it in place.

Here is a basic list I follow in the Northwest. It is by no means complete and I hope you will find treasures of your own to add to it.

- Osiers (also called sticks, branches, or withies)—all varieties of willow, red osier dogwood, chokecherry, raspberry cane, mountain maple, alder, birch, fruit tree prunings, poplar.
- Vines—honeysuckle, grapevine, morning glory.
- Grasses—cattail, bulrush, straw, beargrass, wheat, leaves from gladiolas, lilies, or iris.
- Bark—from alder and birch logs rotted out by the creek, from pine, cedar, or willow peeled in the spring.
- Embellishments—experiment with raw sheep fleece pulled off a barbed wire fence, drippy deer moss hanging on pines, alder berries, pinecones, baby's breath, seeds, etc.

GATHERING AND PREPARATION
Willow:

There are many varieties, but their leaves are generally long and narrow and grow along the entire branch length. Try weeping and pussy willows. The wild growing willow goes by many names. I've heard it called creek, river, or wild willow. It comes in different colors and shades like purple, green, deep red, orange, and golden yellow. The bark often changes colors during the summer months. You may use willow all year 'round, but I prefer winter "stock", for the following reasons:

- The leaves are off, saving the extra step of stripping them, as well as making willow easier to spot in the landscape.
- As the basket dries, it won't loosen up as much as a basket woven in the summer. (However, more willow could be added later.)
- The ground is frozen solid.
- You can store the withies outdoors in nature's freezer. They will stay pliable for weeks. I lay the bundles on the ground in the shade and cover them with snow.
- There are no bugs.

In the winter, look for a feathery red-orange patch of bushes. Try along ditches, rivers, and creeks. I like to collect along the highways. It is noisy, but the road crews occasionally mow the ditches which result in long, branchless willows in a thick patch.

The best baskets I've made were with winter willow dried and resoaked. To soak long willow branches, you can use your bathtub, but willow around here (with the bark on) takes almost two weeks to be pliable. You may prefer to find an alternative "tub":

- Raingutter (see directions in the cattail section).
- Wide plastic sewer pipe with the end cap on, stood on end.
- A temporary trough—I make one with a rectangle of logs or stones and lay about ten feet of heavy vinyl down.
- The pond.
- A fiberglass canoe.

On the last night of soaking, drain the water off to allow the willow to "mellow" overnight. The willow is silky and fragrant, and almost a completely different plant. Winter willow dried and resoaked is well worth the extra effort. (Dried willow can be stored indefinitely.)

In the fall and spring, I find willows break more easily. I suspect it has something to do with the sap coming or going. This problem seems to last just a few weeks. In the spring when the leaves are just beginning, willow is easy to peel. You can save the bark for weaving, too. Dried, peeled willow dyes easily and only needs to soak for about a day. Experiment. To strip the leaves, run a gloved hand down the willow from tip to butt (base). To peel, you can use your fingernails or pull through a notch in a 2 x 4 or fence post.

Another thing that's fun to do with willow is to boil it all day. I take my canner (or big pot) out to the patch and curl up branches inside. Cover with water and simmer all day. While still warm, peel the bark off to reveal "buff" willow. The tannin in the bark dyes the willow.

Red Osier Dogwood

Red osier, (or red twig), dogwood is much more flexible than willow, and without willow's characteristic "kinking". It is not to be confused with a dogwood tree, it grows as a bush. It likes plenty of water, so look along creeks; I find it more plentiful at higher elevations.

The bark is speckled with white dots and is a beautiful red color. The red fades to orange, yellow, and green in the warmer months of spring and summer. In the spring, if one bush is ordinary brown, I cross the road or climb higher and can still find some red twigs. Later in the summer, the bush bears clusters of inedible white berries. In the fall the leaves turn a silvery red.

Unless it's cultivated, it is hard to find long, branchless osiers. But I often find them if I climb into the middle of a tangled bush. I wear protective glasses and a scarf since my long hair will weave itself into the dogwood. (Some days I can really get into my work!)

If you gather during hunting season, take the extra precaution of wearing a bright orange vest and hat. Even then, you may be unseen in a tall patch of cattails or willow. I prefer to avoid that time of year or stay on my own property.

Other Branches:

- Chokecherry—stinky grey bark speckled with white dots.
- Mountain maple—new growth is red. A bush with tiny maple leaves.
- Raspberry cane—pop the thorns off. With gloved hands, run up and down the length.
- Fruit trees—weave within a few days after pruning the orchard—or store in the freezer.

Follow gathering and preparation tips for willow and dogwood.

Cattails and Bulrushes:

Cattails and bulrushes grow in the same type of environment. They are often seen along ponds, lakes, and soggy ditches. From a distance, the leaves of both plants look alike. But the brown spots in the patch will make identification easy. If you see short vertical brown lines, it's cattails. Bulrushes display brown "blobs" on the leaf tip. Up close the difference is more apparent. Cattail leaves are flat and wide, growing from a common stalk. Bulrush leaves are slender, hollow tubes, growing individually.

Long weavers are preferred, so cut rushes (meaning cattails *or* bulrush) at the end of the growing season, around the end of August or early September. They should still be green as sun dried leaves are brittle. To cut bulrush, I use scissors or a pair of pruners. For cattails, the task is easier if you have a long-handled pair of loping shears with a curved blade. The long handles can keep you out of the water as you lean over to cut the leaves at the compressed base. Use the curved blade to pull the stalk within your reach. I try not to cut the flowering stalks so the patch can reseed itself.

When you get the rushes home, they will need to dry out before storage. Otherwise you may have rotted, mildewed, or moldy leaves. Lay a pickup truck's stock racks or the wooden pallets from a warehouse on the ground out of sunlight. Spread the leaves on the wood slats so they can dry thoroughly on both sides. Or lay them directly on the grass and turn them over frequently. Since I live in a dry climate, I do not separate the cattail leaves and have had no problem with mildew. You may need to cut the compressed base off to free the leaves so they can dry individually if your area has high humidity. When the leaves are completely dry, tie up into bundles and store in a cool, dark place.

Weaving freshly cut rushes isn't recommended. They are not very pliable and will also shrink a great deal, resulting in a flimsy basket. However, I once sat by a pretty pond and twined a "garlic" basket from freshly cut bulrush and it didn't turn out too badly. It loosened up a good deal, but it was an opentwined basket anyway, and a little more openness didn't hurt.

To Prepare Dried Rushes For Weaving:

There are two methods:

• Resoak in warm water. This will take from one to three hours. Use your tub or a rain gutter. I purchased a light, plastic rain gutter and snap-on end caps from the hardware store. Use a hack saw to cut the gutter into the desired length—that of your cattails. Soaking in so much water means more shrinkage after they dry than if you use the method described below. But shrinkage can be minimized if you run the leaves through an old wringer to squeeze out excess air and water. I have a very old wooden wringer whose faded print says: "June 20, 1899— Warranted for 3 Years"!

• The preferred method of preparing dried rushes is to let them slowly "mellow". You do this by sprinkling the leaves liberally with water and covering completely under a wet towel. Leave overnight for silky, strong leaves that have minimal shrinkage.
If after your basket is finished you don't like the bright green color, the sun will prematurely age the green to shades of golden browns.

Gladiola, Lilies or Iris:

Use the same methods for rushes.

Honeysuckle:

Honeysuckle is harder to find in the forests in Montana, but it's out there. However I drive down the highway to a friend's mountain home in Idaho. I prefer to gather honeysuckle in the winter months before a snowfall! Some vines grow way up into the trees and are so strong they deform the trunk and will even kill the tree. (The twisted tree trunks make good handles for brooms and backscratchers, so all is not lost!) With a vine that strong, you can imagine how sturdy honeysuckle baskets will be. I like the thin creepers of honeysuckle for most of my weaving projects. Often these vines are hidden under the fallen leaves and you have to feel around with your toes until you can pull one up. Wind the vine in a loose coil the size of a big cooking pot. When you get home, you will need to boil them, and if the coils are the right size, it will save you a lot of struggling. Boil for an hour and let them soak several hours or simmer overnight. Boiling makes the vines stronger and much more pliable. It also makes it very easy to slide the bark off. Remove the bark immediately after boiling and save it to weave with as well as the white-green vine. The peeled honeysuckle can be dyed.

Dry and store indefinitly. To weave, resoak 30 minutes to an hour.

4 ■ TOOLS AND TIPS

TOOLS

When making antler baskets, you will use some of the same tools you needed for previous basket work:

PRUNERS—I prefer by-pass pruners. The curved blade helps me cut a long, tapered angle on ribs.

SCISSORS—To trim cattails and thin reed.

KNIFE—A good sharp blade is indispensable.

AWL, BODKIN, OR THIN SCREWDRIVER

The additional tools needed to weave antler baskets are:

DRILL—I use a hand-held variable speed power drill with a reversible setting. Occasionally a drill bit may be lodged in the antler and putting the drill in reverse makes it easier to remove.

DRILL BITS—Assorted sizes. The hardware store near me has a gizmo with all the available bit sizes drilled out on a "chart". I simply bring small pieces of reed or willow with me and "plug" them in to find the perfect fit. Here is a size chart I use:

ROUND REED	BIT
#2, 3	1/8"
#4	9/64"
#5	5/32"
#6	3/16"
#7	7/32"
#8	17/64"

I use drill bits designed for metal work rather than wood. My favorites are Black & Decker's "Pilot Point".™

GLUE—Wood glue or a glue gun.

LOG—Set on end, it makes a good surface to brace the antler during drilling. The antler's curves can hang over the edge.

BEESWAX—To rub on ribs that need to glide through a hole.

TIPS

Antlers are made of material a little like compressed toe nails. You will notice a strange smell as you begin drilling. Sweep up the shavings to sprinkle as bone meal on your lawn.

To begin a drilled hole, it is helpful to score the antler's surface with a nail or awl. Piercing the slick outer "shell" helps prevent the bit from slipping off the antler. To brace the area that is to be drilled, place it on the upended log, letting the curved area hang over the side. You may prefer to wedge the antler in a vise or clamp, but I find it too awkward and time consuming. With a little practice, you will get the feel of the amount of pressure to exert while drilling as you steady the antler with your other hand.

Placing the drill bit on the score mark, firmly apply pressure and begin the motor. Start the speed slow but sure. Once you have an indentation started, you are pretty safe to speed up the drill. Stop once in awhile to check the hole's progress. Is the hole deep enough? Is the angle correct? The angle can be corrected as you drill. In fact, because of the surface curve or grooves, it may be nearly impossible to start a hole at the right angle. So you may need to begin a little off. Once you have the hole started, bend the drill into the correct position.

When A Wrong Angle Is Drilled:

- Try bending the rib itself into the correct position. Be sure that it is pliable before you start pushing.
- Redrill the same hole, but force a different angle. The hole will be larger than planned, but the rib can be wedged in with a scrap piece of material.
- Change your design!

Not Needing A Drilled Hole Afterall:

- If the hole is in a position to be hidden by the weaving, don't worry about it.
- Plug it with a piece of rib material and sand it off flush.
- Tie a knot in a piece of willow and glue it into the hole. It can be an embellishment. (See photo on page 21).
- Change your design!

Willow knot in hole

Using Antlers For Handles:

- Be sure the size of your basket will be in proportion to the antler. A big, heavy antler will look out of place on a small, dainty creation.
- If the basket will be carried by the antler, be conscientious about putting the rim on securely, passing it through the antler. You may even aim for two rims that pass through the antler, one over the other. Including the antler in rows of weaving can also prevent it from pulling off.
- If you find your antler is too badly damaged from incorrect drilling, it can be cut on a table saw into buttons, toggles, or forked ends that can be attached to a basket as a decorative accent.

Tips For Weaving The Frame:

As you're weaving the frame, you may realize the shape isn't quite what you had planned. The length of the ribs can be adjusted in the same way you would adjust for a regular ribbed basket. However, if the rib needing adjustment is one that is permanently fitted into the antler, you will need to use one of these methods:

- Too long a rib—Cut it off at a long tapered point near the last rows of weaving. Insert the rib back into the weaving, letting it lay alongside the other cut rib.

• If the rib is too short—This gets more complicated. Find a place where the too-short rib meets up with an added rib. Work your pruners in between the weavers and cut the rib off at the place the added rib begins. (See photo below.)

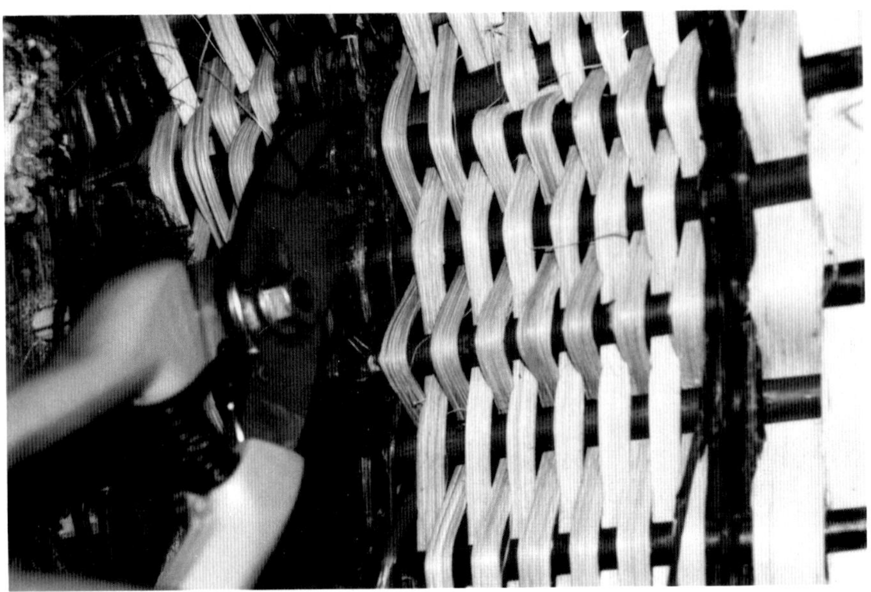

• Slide the rib out carefully to the position you prefer. The *added* rib should look like it was the original one into the antler, and the *adjusted* rib is now masquerading as the added rib.

Tips For Weight Compensation

The antler is usually heavier than the basket, and it may cause the basket to roll off balance. Here are some suggestions to compensate:

• Try weaving a flatter bottom frame such as a tube basket or the basket pictured on page 48.

• Add an antler chip to a rib. Drill one hole in the edge of an antler button, large enough to insert the rib. Slide the chip along the rib until it stops the basket from rolling over. (See photo below.)

• If the basket has a curly border (Chapter 7, page 41), use a cluster of curls inserted into the weaving on the bottom of the basket. This will be like a little pedestal.
• Lash a piece of antler onto the bottom—Take a smaller antler (or forked end) and place it under the basket where it steadies the roll. Mark the position and drill a series of small holes in the antler. Lash it on to the basket with #2 or #3 round reed, or willow.
• Put a weight (stone) inside your finished basket.

5 ■ TUBE BASKETS

Moose horn with reed

A tube basket is a good project to begin with. It will work best with a straight or just slightly curved antler. They are good baskets for magazines, kindling, rolled up bath towels, or a pillow inside for a pet bed. They are easy to make in all different sizes, mostly depending on the antler you have to work with. A large basket can hold folded quilts or afghans. A small one may fit a stack of dinner napkins. The sides can be curved upwards to hold a pile of potatoes, or balls of yarn.

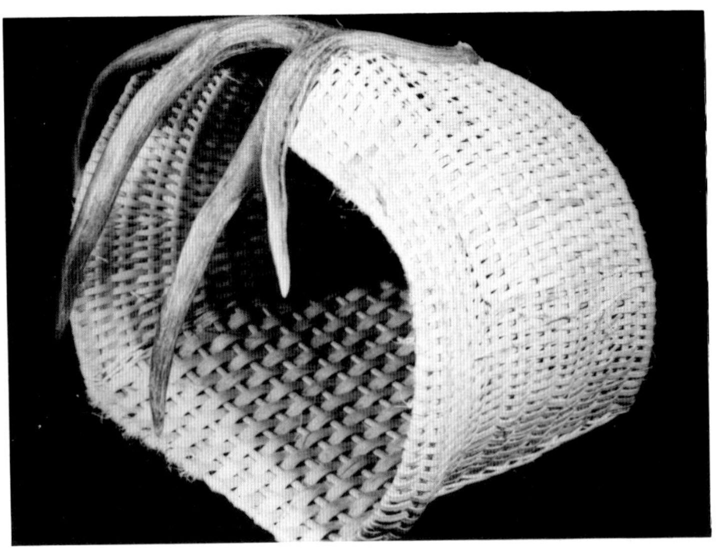

Deer antler and reed

In this tube basket, the antler resembles a long skinny hand reaching over the top. The three rod wale (or "triple weave") edge along the bottom is visible in the lower right corner. This gives a crisp upset and a defined, flat surface to sit nicely.

MAKING A TUBE BASKET

Materials:
- Rib material—Either willow rods or round reed. I also use oval/oval reed.
- Base weavers—I like something wider than my sides. 3/8", 1/2", or 5/8" flat reed. Whatever you have on hand or prefer will work fine.
- Side weavers—Your preference here, too. It could be a thin flat reed like 1/4" or a small round reed such as #3 or #2. Or use materials you gather yourself.

Equipment:
- Cutters—pruners, knives, and scissors.
- Power drill
- Drill bit—the diameter of your rib material.

- Good glue—a gun or waterproof wood glue.
- A board or screw block

STEP 1: Drilling your horn

The holes should be no further apart than ½ an inch, even if it's a big basket. Drill holes along both sides. There should be an equal number of holes on both sides. Redrill some holes completely through the narrowest section.

STEP 2: Determining the length of your ribs

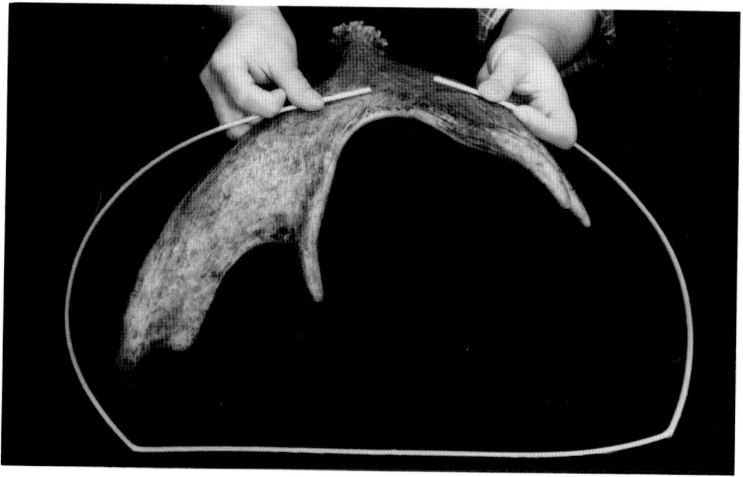

STEP 3: Cutting your ribs

Cut the same number of ribs as you have holes drilled on one side. Use the measurement from Step 2. If you want the front and back bottom edge to curve upwards, cut four extra ribs.

STEP 4: Weaving your base

Lay out your ribs using a screwblock or board to give some semblance to the disorder. Taper your base weaver if you are using wide reed. Weave over and under wrapping an extra turn on the end ribs. Weave across the base. Don't worry about the ribs being uneven. When you let the base dry, it will be fairly simple to pull the ribs through the weave until you have the same amount protruding on either end of the base.

STEP 5: Inserting the ribs into the horn

First, do you want a sharp upset at the base? If so, soak your base and bend the ribs at the edge of the wide weaving. This is easier if you pinch the reed ribs with pliers where the bend will be, or for willow ribs, insert a knife's point just past the bark and twist slightly. Do this on the inside bend. Triple twine (Three-rod wale) at the upset if desired.

Roughly place the ribs in the corresponding holes. The holes through the narrow area of the antler allows ribs to pass each other and come out the other side. This is to decrease the possibility of the antler pulling off should anyone try to lift the basket by the horn. The ribs will probably need to be tapered thinner to allow both ribs to pass each other inside the antler.

Cut the other ribs to the length needed for a nice shape and insert into the remaining holes. Putting the ribs in roughly at first helps to hold the antler over the work so you can see the shape that's developing. When you are satisfied with the basket's shape, glue all the ribs in their holes.

STEP 6: Weaving the sides

Start at the antler and weave down each side with your choice of weaving material. Fill in when necessary. ("filling in" goes by other names such as "packing" or "turning back". This compensates for the different length in ribs.)

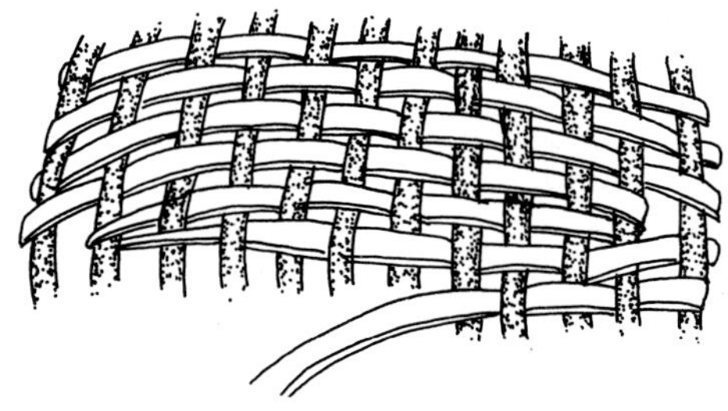

When you turn back on a rib, a triangular space develops (right hand side). Improve your turning back by trimming the width of the weaver (left hand side).

This horn posed a problem. The tapered end curved back more than usual. So I drilled a hole for a rib to pass through on its way up to the main holes. This made the side hug closer to the antler and it became a more integral part of the basket.

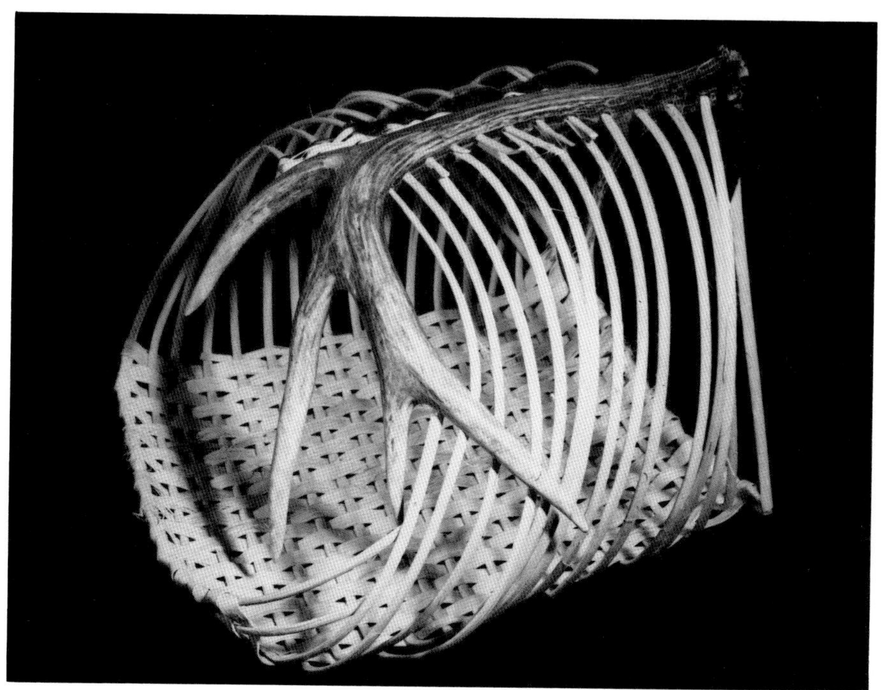

The tapered end curved back so much I had another problem. The inside curve at the top wasn't as long as the curve on the other side, so I couldn't drill as many holes. I was short one hole and a rib had no where to go. I could have cut it like the two short front ribs, but instead I drilled another hole in front of the rib that passes through the tapered end.

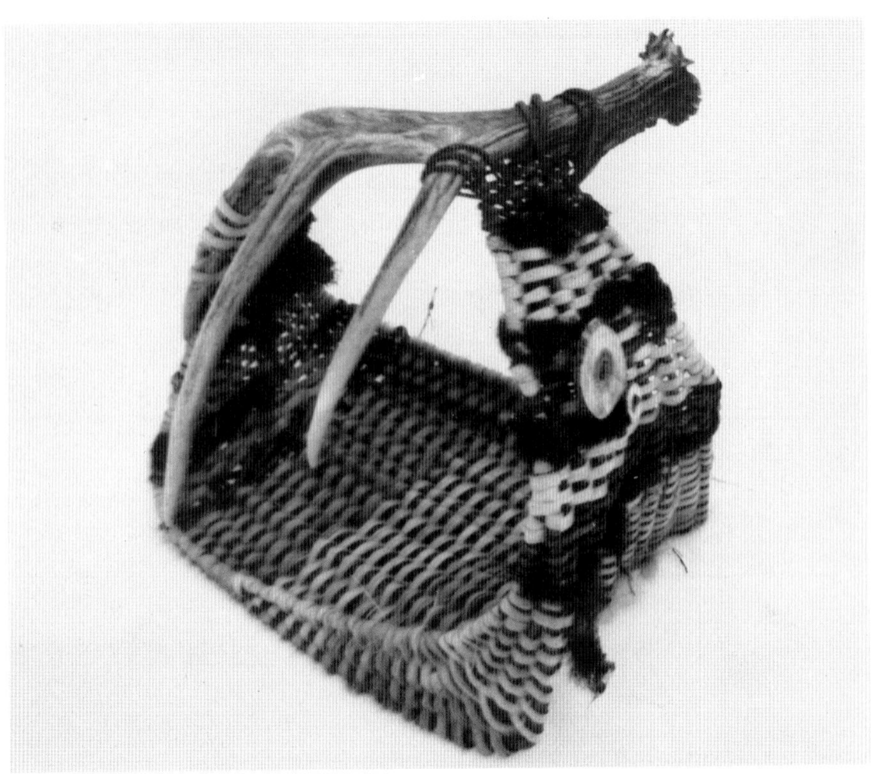

This tube basket was made much differently. The side you can't see is a fork handled in the same way as the egg basket's fork on page 49. This tube basket is made of willow ribs and weavers, deer moss and reed.

Mule deer antler with reed.

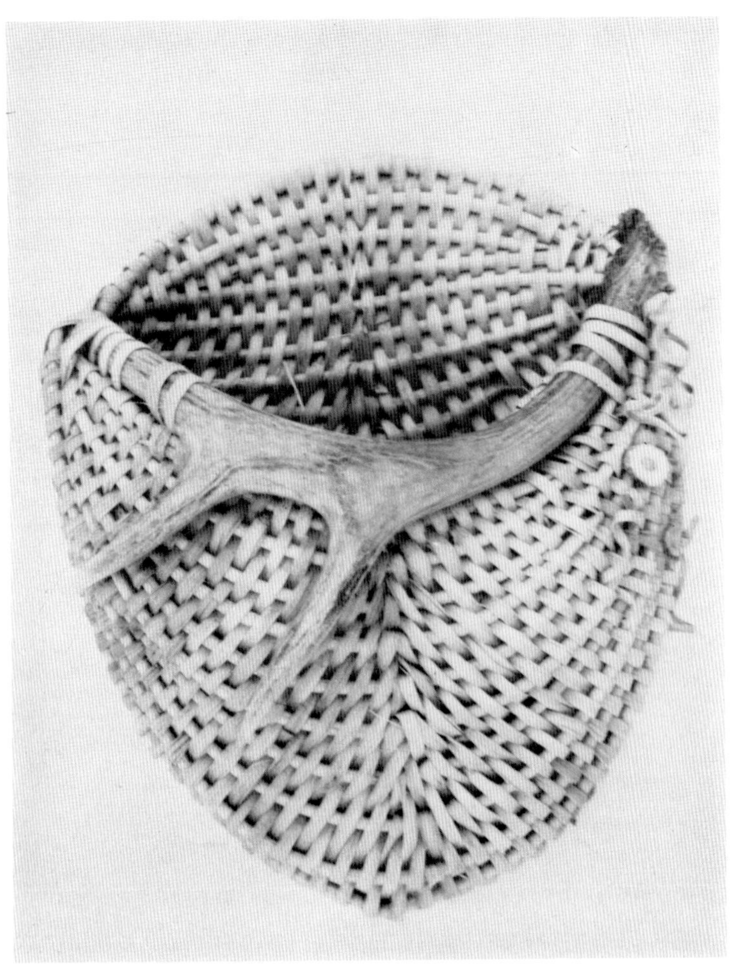

Wall Pockets are such useful vessels! They will obligingly hold kitchen utensils, scissors and pens, toothpaste and brushes, mail, matches, hair combs and hair brushes. Larger sizes can keep your magazines, washcloths, potatoes, bottles of lotions, or mail. Of course, they could just be a nice place to put a bunch of dried flowers.

The antler on this wall pocket was a nice weathered grey. So I dyed the reed pale grey to match and stuck the whole thing in a dark plastic bag until it had just the right amount of mildew! The speckles of deep black aged the reed as old as the horn.

Front and back views of another wall pocket. Some of the front ribs pass through holes drilled in the longest tapered end, front and center. Those are strange little pine cones on the side. I use goat lacing tied through the weaving for a hanging hook.

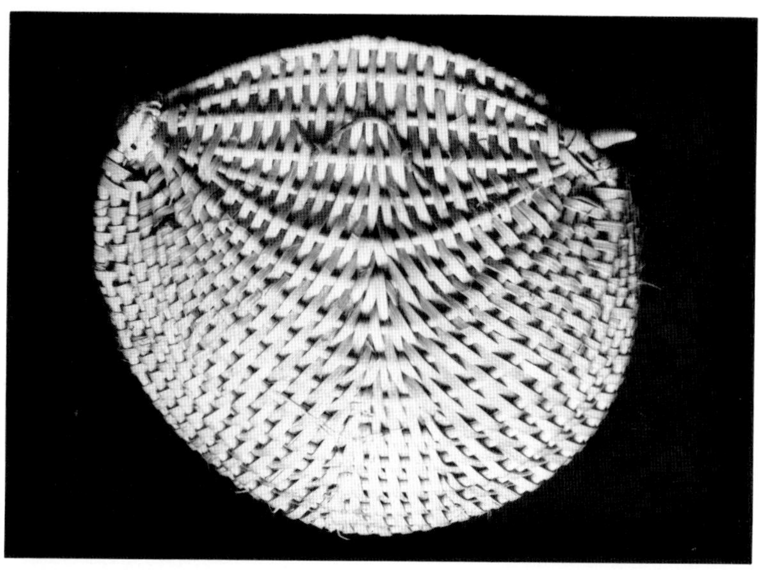

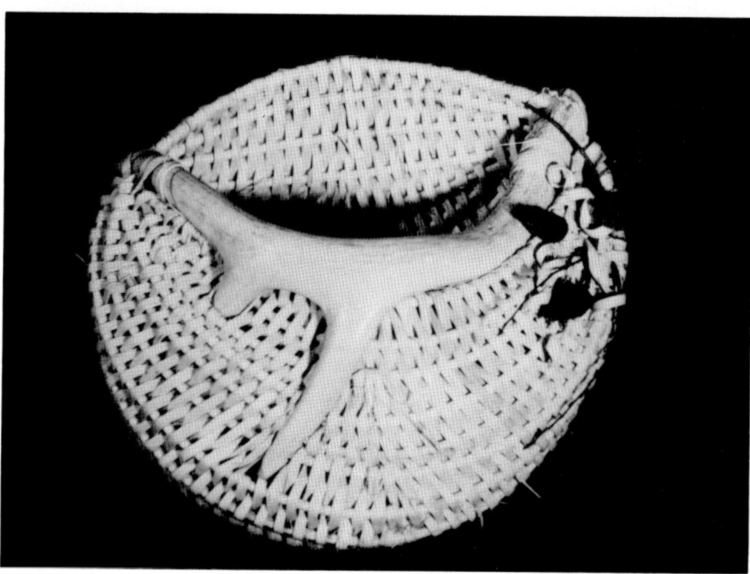

This is how most of my wall pockets begin. Ribs pass through the tapered end and enter a deep hole in the shed end. The shed end gets many holes drilled in for the other starting ribs, while the tapered end usually has a few ribs resting on the horn until they are woven in place. Notice the "staple" on the inside center of the antler. Two holes were drilled—not completely through—and a bent piece of rib material was glued into position. It's purpose is to keep the basket snug up against the antler.

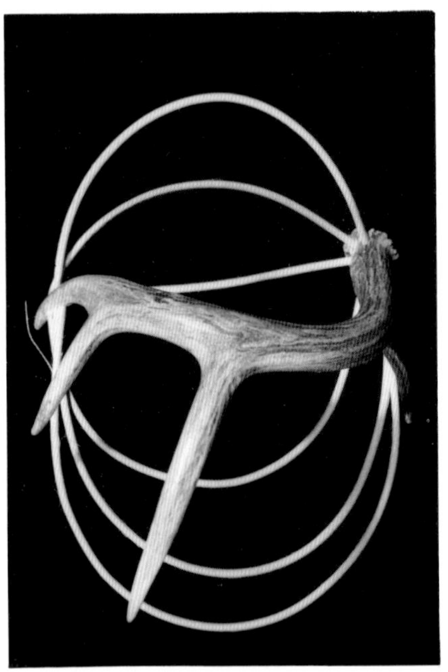

Front

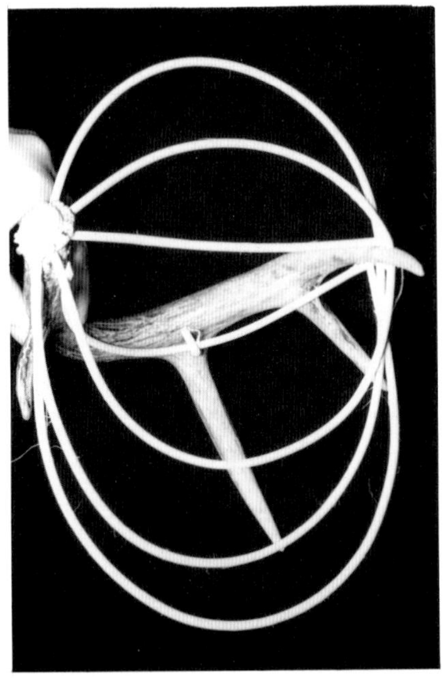

Back

Looking down into a wall pocket. The protruding tapered end could still be sliced off on a table saw and the remnant cut further for buttons. Very curved antlers are usually from a white tail, while mule deer grow their horns a little straighter.

A pocket made with a mule deer antler may be thinner, but will still be ideal for plenty of storage.

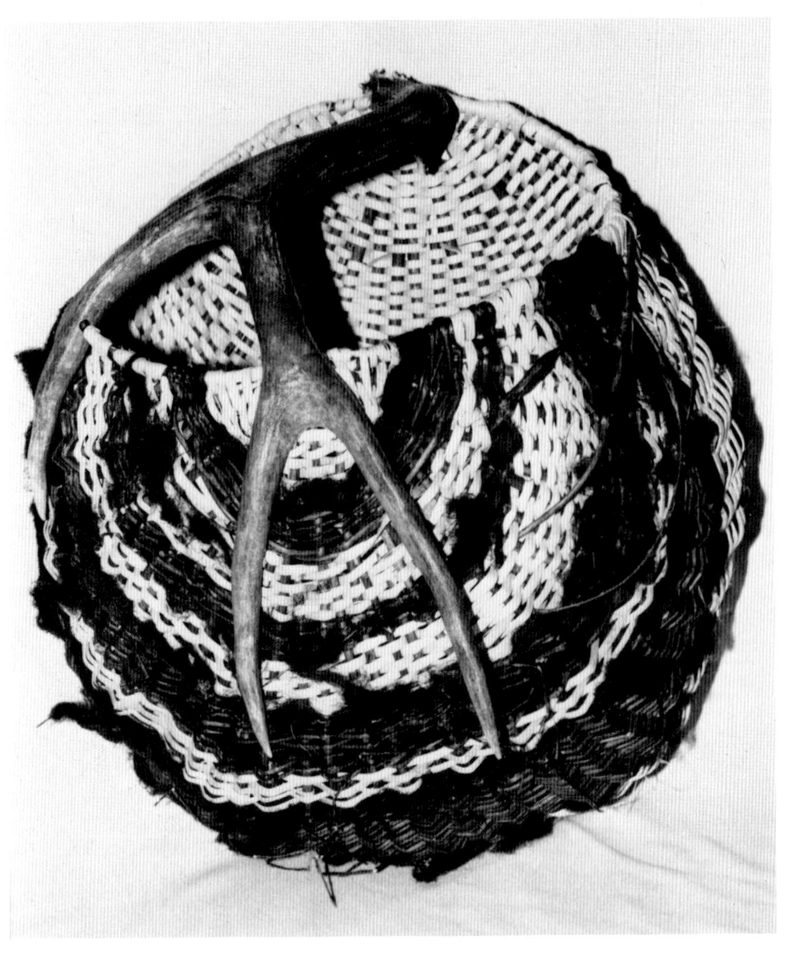

Dimensions: 20" x 23" with a 19" opening.

This is a very large wall pocket woven with willow ribs and weavers, deer moss, and reed. The rim rib passes completely through the horn to support the weight of the contents. After all the work in weaving a special basket, you wouldn't want the antler to come off!

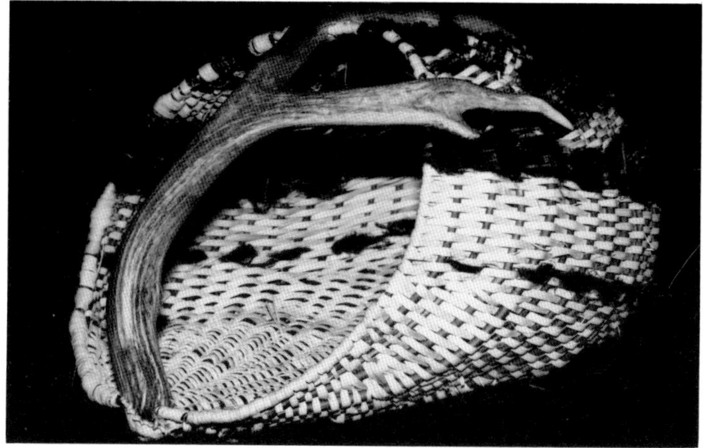

This shows the same basket on its back. It is used as a floor or table basket in this position.

This is one way of dealing with the antler's forks. The more you drill and insert a tightly fitting rib, the more your basket will be a part of the antler and not something just "tacked" on. Holes through the prongs are for weavers to pass through and keep the basket snuggled up to the antler.

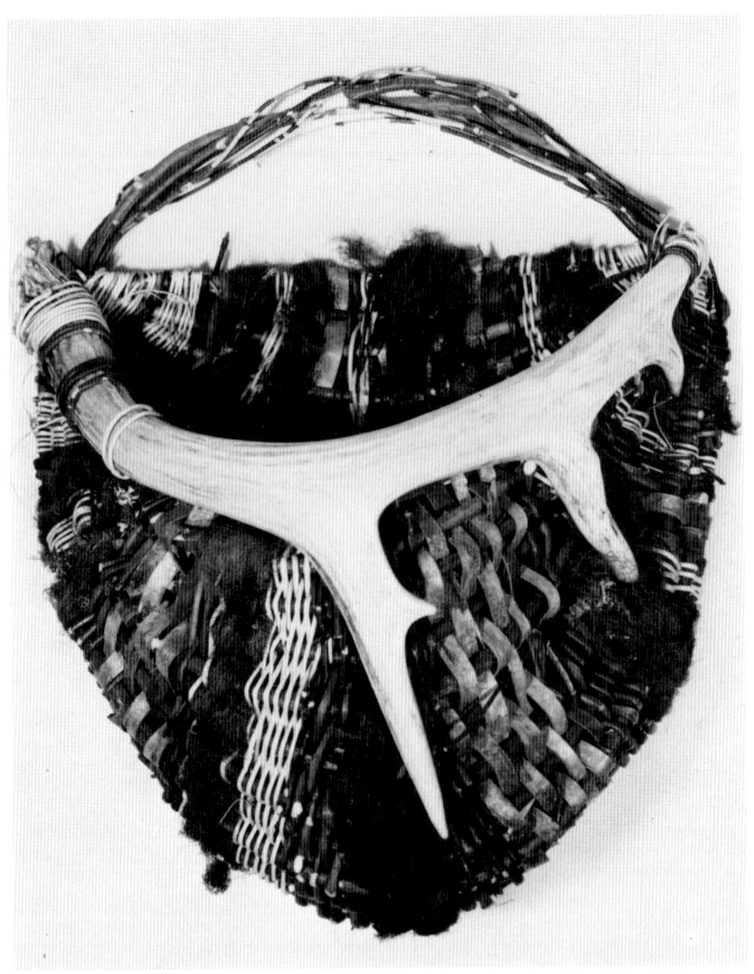

This basket has hung by our fireplace for a long time. It is made entirely from mountain gleanings. The thin white material is boiled and peeled honeysuckle. The fluff is deer moss. Alder bark is cut into wide strips. The ribs, handle and some weavers are red osier dogwood. I collected these things from a single mountain on a very nice hike.

Sometimes my friends won't go anywhere with me unless I leave my pruners and knife at home. But my sister Laura didn't mind me popping out of the car and into the bushes while we were waiting at a "drive thru" once!

7 ■ EGG BASKETS

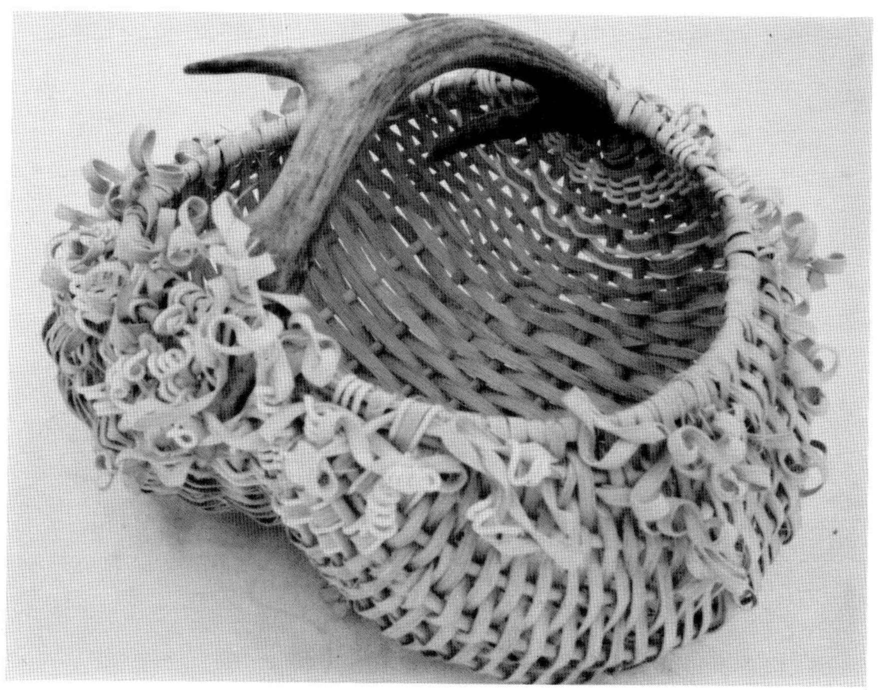

Curls from 3/16″ flat and #2 round reed.

There are many ways to attach a rim to an antler. So much depends on the curves and thickness of the horn itself, that you have to be flexible when you start. Most of the time I find small white tail deer antlers that are fairly uniform and this is the way my frame starts.

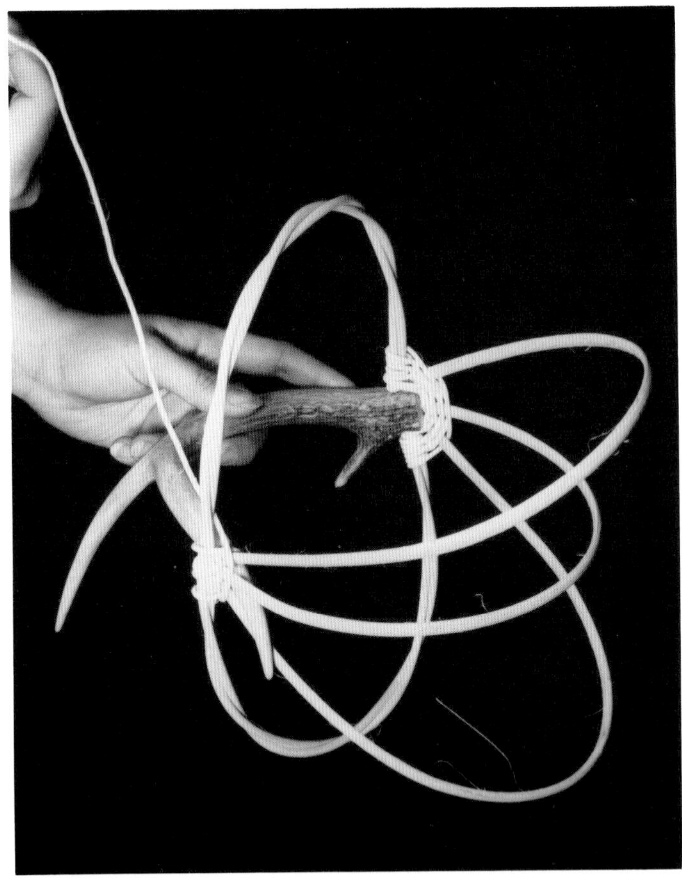

Keep in mind that in ribbed baskets, you do not have to start an intersection with a big lashing to hold many ribs. Ribs can be added with very little to hold them in place if you have a good hand on them while weaving with the other. One at first, then two ribs, etc. (If you add ribs in pairs, near each other, you won't mess up the weaving pattern for very long.)

WHITE TAIL ANTLER BASKET

Take into consideration the size of your antler when you begin an egg basket. This one would have had nicer proportions if I had made the basket larger. But you live and learn, and after all, it still served a function. Antlers from white tail deer have a sharp curve, making tall handles.

The tapered end:

Because this antler was flat on the "wrong" side, I couldn't drill
a hole for the rim rib. So I used a small bit (1/8"), and drilled four
holes. Using #2 bleached round reed, (more flexible) I "sewed" the rim
on and began weaving the ribs in place with the same piece.

The shed end:

It took me a lot of baskets before I found this very easy way of starting. Just insert the ribs and glue, and start weaving. If the shed end is curved too much, you may have to drill into the wide end and forgo the knob showing.

(Cutaway view for drilling holes)

OFF CENTERED EGG BASKET

The rim rib on this basket fits through holes drilled in all three tapered ends, and enters deep holes on either side of the shed end. You can see the willow plug in a hole I decided not to use. An antler slice passes through a rib at the bottom to keep the basket from rolling over.

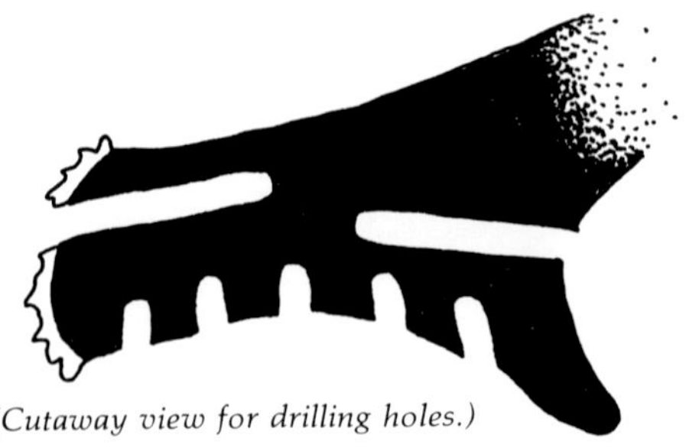

(Cutaway view for drilling holes.)

Looking into the basket.

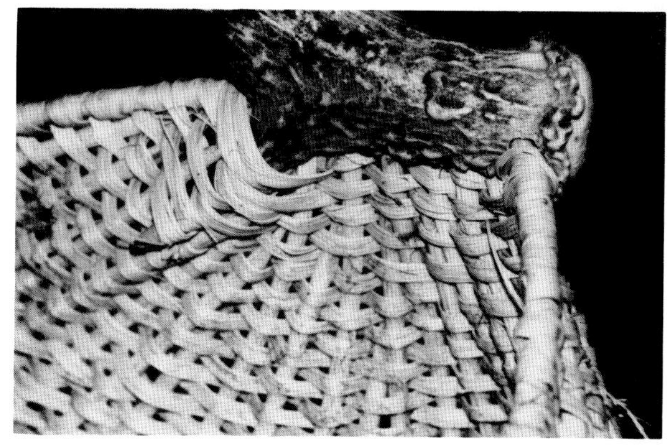

View from the inside.

EGG BASKET WITH A WILLOW FORK

This antler wasn't naturally shed so the end was polished on a belt sander. It has willow ribs, and reed, deer moss and more willow for weavers. There was no need to add a piece of antler on the bottom for weight compensation as the ribs were bent to make a wide flat surface.

Holes were drilled in the crotch of the fork. The willow was woven in first, then the rim was lashed on like some potatoe baskets. The rim goes through the shed end which was started in the same manner as on page 45.

(Cutaway view for drilling holes).

ELK BASKETS

Elk Horn with reed, cattails, and willow.

Elk antlers have a long prong shooting out from the shed end. You may need to lay the prong horizontally:

For a basket secure to the Elk Antler, I use this method:

Drilling:
Shed end: four holes completely through.

Tapered end: three holes completely through. Two holes are
drilled only partway into the antler, one on the top left side, and
one on the lower right.

Inserting ribs: Using the longest length of round reed available, and
beginning with a "partway" hole, thread the reed around and around
until you reach the other "partway" hole. If you run short of reed, add a
new length by tapering the two ends inside the antler.

White tail deer antler and reed.

THE FRAME:

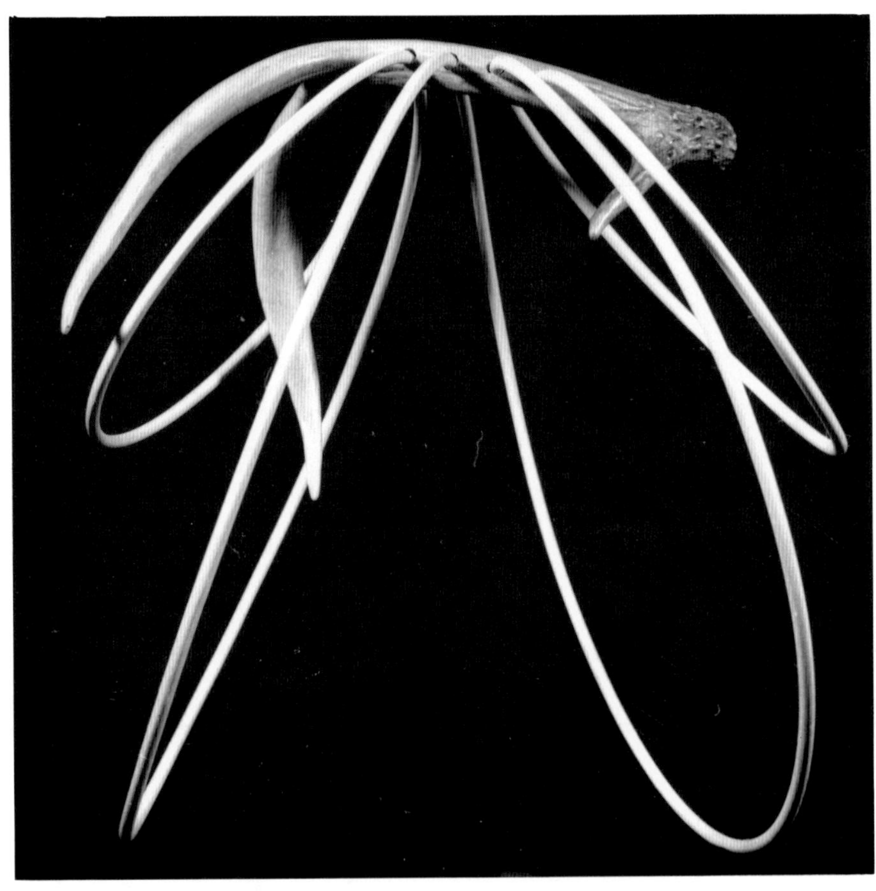

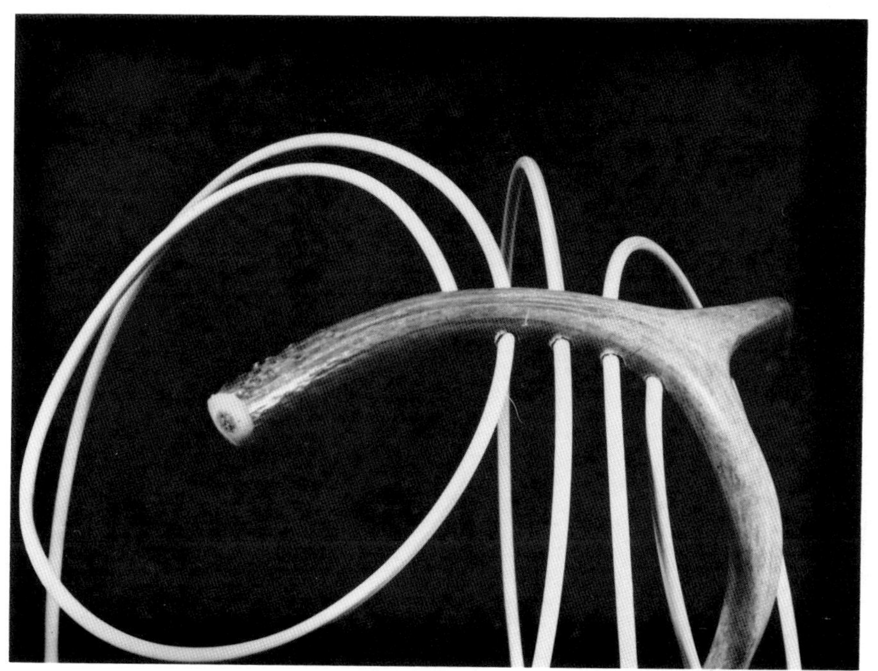

I use a very long piece of #7 round reed so I can make a continuous spring of ribs. This will keep the basket secure to the antler.

Drill three holes completely through about ½″ apart. Drill a fourth hole just partway on opposite ends of the row of three. Start the reed in a partway hole and thread it around and around the main three holes. End it in the remaining part-way hole. Spread out the circles and weave as you would a normal hen basket, adding more ribs as necessary.

On this hen basket, three main holes were drilled completely through. Three partway holes are added to the wider curve. The three ribs on the small curve were woven in first so the extra ribs from the other side could curve around and be inserted into the weaving.

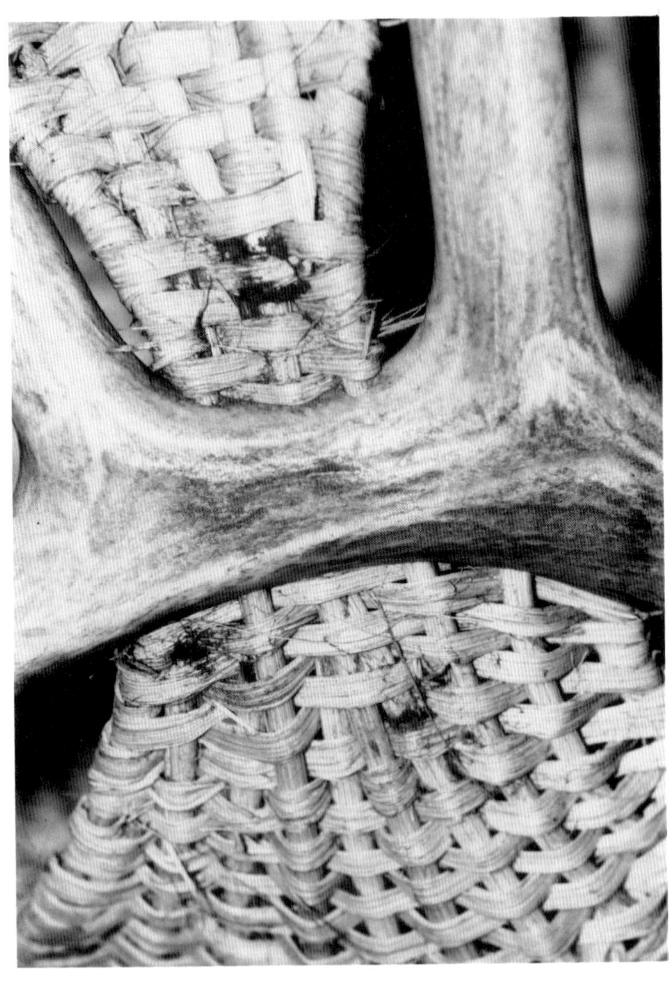

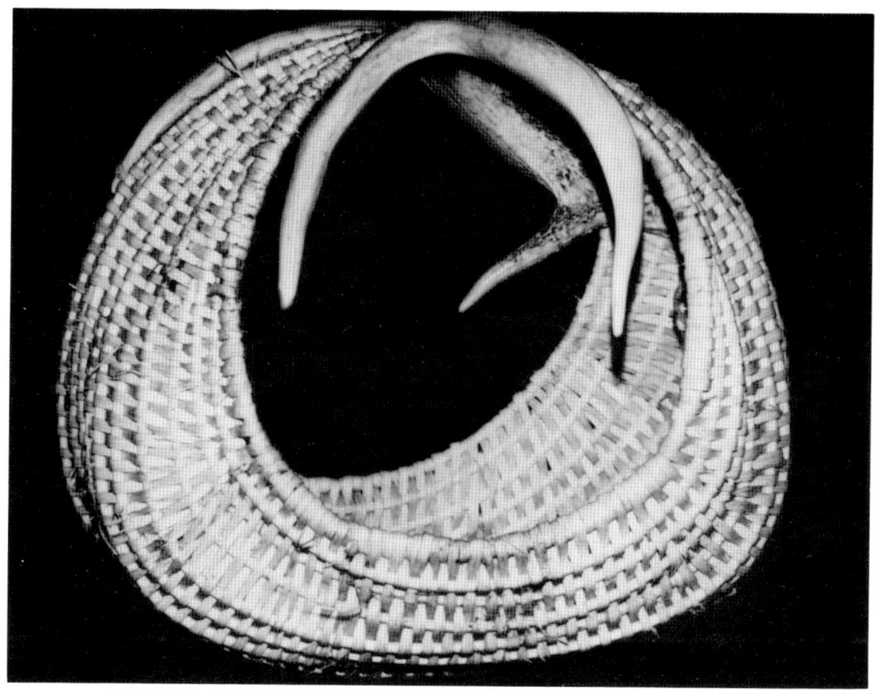

A nice finish on a brown antler basket is a matching stain. I like Watco Danish Oil finish. It is non-toxic after it cures which is important to me for food storage. I buy the strongest shade and dilute it to the desired color with mineral oil from the drug store. Brush it on very lightly.

You may also experiment with staining the antler itself. Very bleached, weathered antlers can be dyed.

The ribs may give the illusion of passing completely through the shed end, but in reality they are shorter pieces beginning or ending inside the antler. Drilling the correct angle in the shed end is crucial, although some allowance can be made by slightly bending a flexible rib.

Detail of rib insertion.

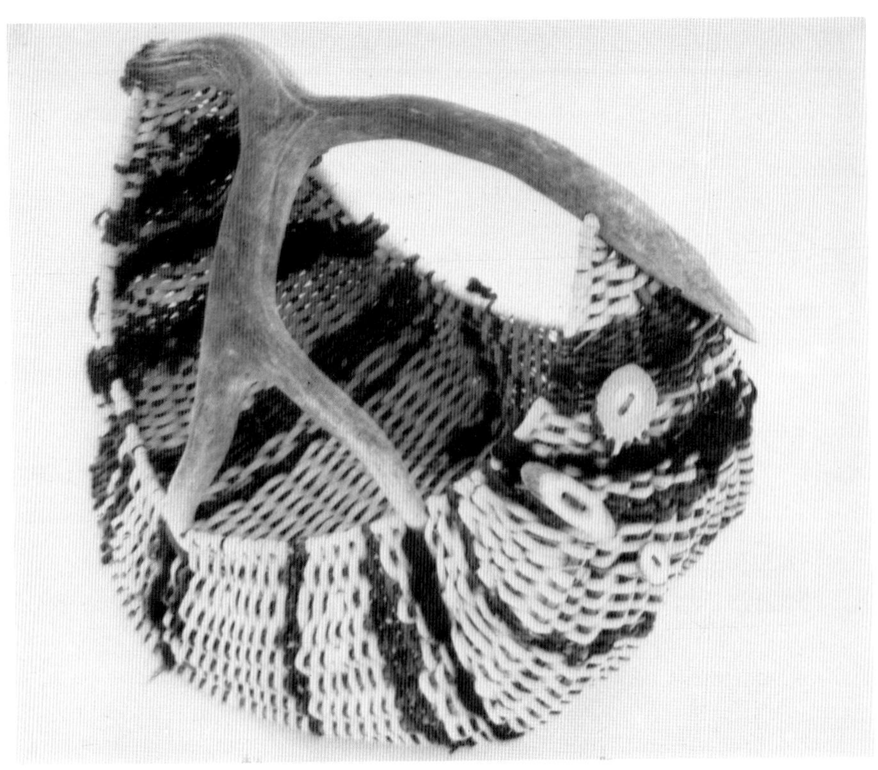

Mule deer antler.

This hen basket was constructed similiar to the egg baskets in chapter 7. The rim rib passes through all four points. It is made of red osier dogwood, "deer moss," (lichen) and reed. Antler buttons are sewn on with willow.

■ BIBLIOGRAPHY

Irwin, John Rice. *Baskets and Basketmakers in Southern Appalachia,* 1982. Shiffer Publishing Ltd., Box E, Exton, Pennsylvania 19341.

Barratt, Olivia Elton. *Rushwork,* 1986. Dryad Press Ltd., 4 Fitzhardinge Street, London, England W1HOAH.

Lumpkin, Beryl Omega. *From Vines to Vessels,* 1987. The Overmountain Press, Johnson City, Tennessee 37601.

Heseltine, Alastair. *Baskets and Basketmaking,* 1982. Shire Publications Ltd., Cromwell House, Church Street, Princes Risborough, Aylesbury, Bucks, England HP17-9AJ, UK.

■ TO "TALK SHOP" IN MONTANA:

- Joseph's Coat
  131 W. Main
  Missoula, MT 59802
  (406) 549-1419

- The Cottage
  351 River Street
  Big Fork, MT 59911
  (406) 837-6301

- Bernina Craft Center
  912—13th Ave. South
  Great Falls, MT 59405
  (406) 452-7222

- Red Barn Baskets
  4741 White Street
  Missoula, MT 59802
  (406) 728-2878

- McCoys Arts and Crafts
  1212 Grand Ave.
  Billings, MT 59100
  (406) 252-1043